# Timeline of the Titanic

### Summer 1907
Lord Pirrie and J. Bruce Ismay decide to build *Titanic* and her two sister ships.

### 31 March 1909
*Titanic*'s keel is laid down in Belfast, Ireland (now Northern Ireland).

### 3 April 1912
*Titanic* arrives in Southampton. Over the next week, supplies, cargo and coal are loaded aboard.

### 31 March 1912
Fitting-out of *Titanic* is completed.

### 29 July 1908
The design for *Titanic* is approved.

### 31 March 1911
The hull of the *Titanic* is launched.

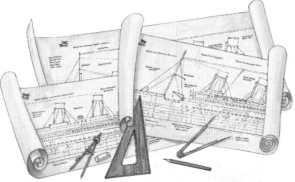

### 2 April 1912
*Titanic* passes her sea trials and leaves Belfast for Southampton, England, that evening.

## 12 April 1912

By now, *Titanic* has covered 623 km (387 miles).

## 14 April 1912

*Titanic*'s starboard bow strikes an iceberg below the waterline. *Titanic* begins to take on water.

## 10 April 1912

*Titanic* leaves Cherbourg, France.

## 6 April 1912

Majority of *Titanic*'s crew is recruited.

## 13 April 1912

First warning of heavy ice.

## 11 April 1912

*Titanic* sets sail across the Atlantic Ocean.

## 15 April 1912

*Titanic* sinks.

# Map of shipwrecks around the world

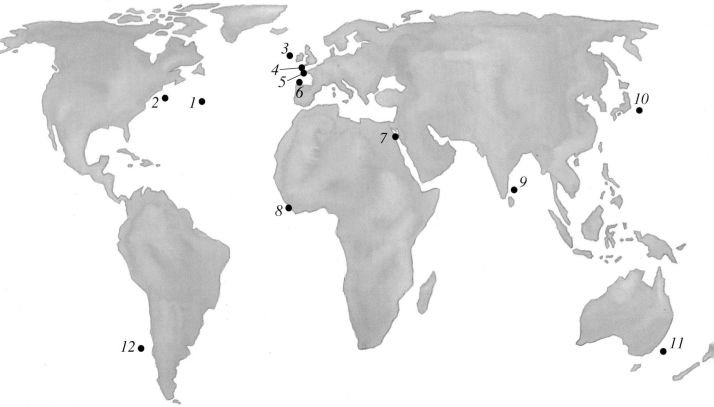

**1** The *Titanic*.

**2** The *Andrea Doria* hit the *Stockholm* and sank off New York in 1956.

**3** In 1915 a German U-boat sank the unarmed liner *Lusitania*. Almost 1,200 people died.

**4** In 1922, the P&O ship *Egypt* collided with another ship in fog and sank.

**5** The liner *Prins Frederik* sank off the Bay of Biscay in 1890.

**6** In 1852 the *Amazon* caught fire and sank in the Bay of Biscay on its maiden voyage.

**7** The P&O steamship *Carnatic* hit a reef in the Red Sea in 1869, but most of its cargo was salvaged.

**8** In 1862, the *Cleopatra*, carrying gold dust and coins, sank in the currents of a river in Sierra Leone.

**9** P&O steamship *Malabar*, loaded with 1,080 boxes of gold bullion, sank off Sri Lanka in 1860.

**10** The *Asiatic Prince* and 2 tonnes (2.2 tons) of gold disappeared in 1928 between Los Angeles, California, and Japan.

**11** Strong winds blew the *Catterthun* onto rocks off Australia in 1895. The ship carried gold sovereigns worth £11,000 – millions of pounds in today's money.

**12** In 1892, the steamship *John Elder* and its cargo of gold and silver were lost off Chile.

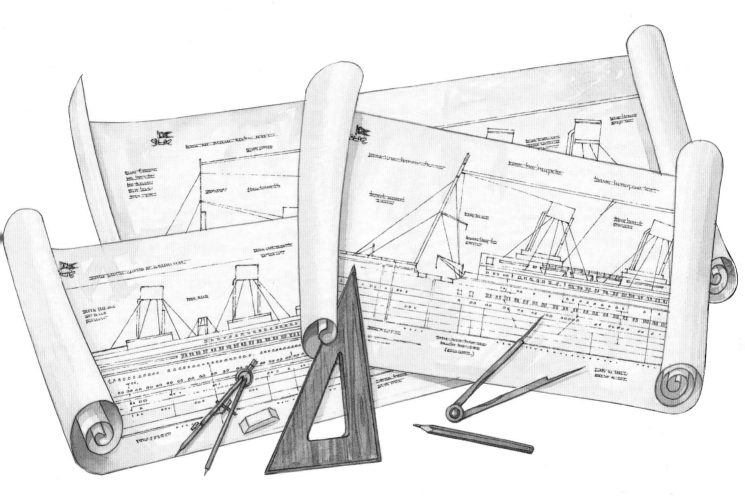

*Author:*
**David Stewart** has written many non-fiction books for children, including *You Wouldn't Want to Be an Egyptian Mummy!* He lives in Brighton with his wife and son.

*Artist:*
**David Antram** was born in Brighton, England, in 1958. He studied at Eastbourne College of Art and then worked in advertising for 15 years before becoming a full-time artist. He has illustrated many children's non-fiction books.

*Series creator:*
**David Salariya** was born in Dundee, Scotland. He has illustrated a wide range of books and has created and designed many new series for publishers both in the UK and overseas. In 1989 he established The Salariya Book Company. He lives in Brighton with his wife, illustrator Shirley Willis, and their son, Jonathan.

*Editor:*
**Karen Barker Smith**

Published in Great Britain in MMXIV by
Book House, an imprint of
The Salariya Book Company Ltd
25 Marlborough Place, Brighton BN1 1UB
www.salariya.com
www.book-house.co.uk

PB ISBN: 978-1-909645-72-1

© The Salariya Book Company Ltd MMXIV

1 3 5 7 9 8 6 4 2

A CIP catalogue record for this book is available from the British Library.

Printed and bound in China.

Visit our website at www.book-house.co.uk
or go to www.salariya.com for **free** electronic versions of:
**You Wouldn't Want to be an Egyptian Mummy!**
**You Wouldn't Want to be a Roman Gladiator!**
**You Wouldn't Want to be a Polar Explorer!**
**You Wouldn't Want to sail on a 19th-Century Whaling Ship!**

PAPER FROM SUSTAINABLE FORESTS

# You Wouldn't Want to™ Sail on the Titanic!

Written by
## David Stewart

Illustrated by
## David Antram

Created and designed by
## David Salariya

# One Voyage You'd Rather Not Make

BOOK HOUSE
*a* SALARIYA *imprint*

# Contents

# Introduction

The year is 1907. Your name is J. Bruce Ismay and you are the managing director of the White Star Line, a shipping company. Your main rival, Cunard, has just launched the passenger liner *Lusitania*. At 241 metres long, she is huge and very fast. At a London dinner party with William Pirrie, you discuss the highly lucrative sea route between Europe and the United States. Lord Pirrie is a director of Harland and Wolff, the Belfast-based shipbuilders who have built all of White Star's vessels. You decide to think big and plan to build three ships that are heavier than the *Lusitania's* 30,000 tonnes and 30 m longer. With luxurious and speedy transatlantic crossings you will attract the wealthy passenger trade and the growing number of emigrants travelling to North America.

On 10 April 1912, at 12.00 noon, the *Titanic* will leave Southampton, England, on her maiden voyage. The ship will set out to cross the Atlantic Ocean and plans to arrive in New York seven days later. She is the largest ship in the world and, for her wealthy First-Class passengers, certainly the most luxurious. At this point, you definitely want to sail on the *Titanic*. Little do you know that the ship is sailing towards disaster...

# Designing the Titanic

*J. Bruce Ismay*

I have a dream, to build three ships more luxurious than the world has ever seen.

The architects and draughtsmen at the Harland and Wolff shipyard work hard to make the planned superliners a reality. While the plans for the ships are drawn up, three dry docks are converted into two – no existing dry dock is large enough to build the huge new liners! On 29 July 1908, the plans are ready. The keel plate for *Olympic*, the first of the three giant liners, is laid on 16 December 1908. The keel plate for the second liner is laid three months later on 31 March 1909. Her name is *Titanic*.

You were born in Liverpool, England, in 1862. Your father founded the White Star Shipping Line in 1869. In 1902, the White Star Line was sold to American financier J. P. Morgan but you stayed on as managing director.

Although *Olympic* and *Titanic* were almost identical in size, *Titanic* was actually 1,004 tonnes heavier than her sister ship.

The third ship, *Gigantic*, was later renamed *Britannic*.

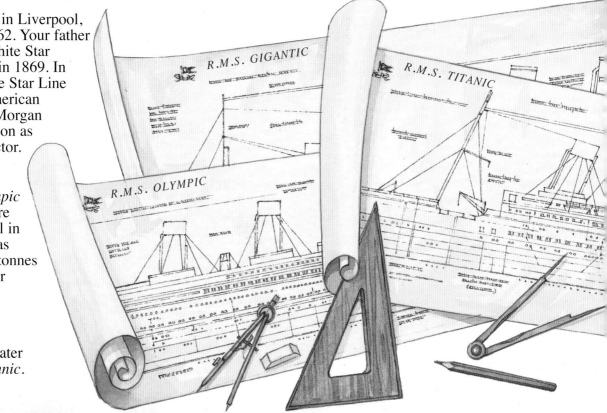

## Titanic's specifications

Ship weight: 47,070 gross registered tonnes.
Hull weight: 29,586 tonnes.
Length: 269 m.
Width: 28 m.
Anchors: Three, with a total weight of 36 tonnes.
  Each chain link weighs about 80 kg.
Rudder weight: 9,185 kg.
Boilers: 29, each weighing over 100 tonnes.
Propellers: Three – one measuring 5 m across
  and two others, each measuring 7 m across.
Funnels: Four, but only front three in use. Stern
  funnel used for ventilation.
Cost: Completed ship cost £1,300,000 in 1912.

### Handy hint

You have designed one ship, so you might as well use the same design for two more.

How many passengers and crew on board?

Regulations state that the ship must carry lifeboats for 962 people. We have an extra four collapsible boats – room for 1,178 people.

We have room for 3,511 people.

7

# Building the 'unsinkable' ship

**Y**ou have the plans, you have the dry dock and now you need workers. The shipyard employs approximately 11,300 men to build *Titanic*. The central girders are first riveted to the keel to make the spine of the hull. Then 350 steel frames, with 10 levels of deck supports, form the skeleton of the ship. Bulkheads divide *Titanic*'s hull into 16 compartments, which are said to be watertight because each extends well above the waterline. The ship could still float even if four of the compartments were filled with water! The shipyard is a dangerous place to work. Eight workers have been killed during construction and over 240 accidents have been recorded by Harland and Wolff.

*Aaah!*

**RIVETERS.** They rivet steel plates, up to 2 m high and 11 m wide, weighing 5 tonnes, to the frames.

**ANCHORS.** *Titanic* needs three anchors. The heaviest weighs over 17 tonnes and will need a team of 20 horses to pull it from the foundry to the shipyard.

# Launched but not completed

n 31 May 1911, *Titanic*'s empty hull slides down the slipway. Sixty-two seconds later she enters the water for the first time. According to the custom of the shipyard and the White Star Line, the ship is launched unchristened.

Launch
OF
White Star Royal Mail
Triple-Screw Steamer
'TITANIC'
At Belfast,
Wednesday, 31st May, 1911, at 12.15 p.m.
Admit Bearer

Launch invitation

## Who's who?

**Chief Engineer**  **Electrician**  **Boiler maker**

**Fireman**  **Stoker**  **Trimmer**

**Greaser**  **Apprentice**

BOILER ROOMS. Seventy-three trimmers (who break up coal into small lumps) and 177 firemen work in the boiler rooms.

10

DOWN THE SLIPWAY. To get the massive ship down to the water, over 23 tonnes of soap, grease and train oil are used. *Titanic* slides almost 550 m before being brought to a halt by six anchor chains and two other piles of chains weighing 80 tonnes each.

Handy hint

Yaaawwn

If you want a job as a stoker, wait at the dock just before the ship sets sail. Casual labour is hired at the last minute as replacements for any crew members who fail to turn up.

All the machinery, including the engines, boilers and funnels, is installed on board once the ship is afloat by using floating cranes. Once this is completed the vessel can be towed away to a fitting-out berth. *Titanic*'s interior will take 10 months and several million man-hours to complete. On 2 April 1912, the completed *Titanic* sets sail to begin her sea trials.

11

# Captain and crew

Captain Edward John Smith has been commodore of the White Star fleet since 1904. As he usually commands the White Star's newest ship, he will take charge of *Titanic* on her maiden voyage. Captain Smith is popular with his passengers and crew. Some wealthy passengers refuse to sail across the Atlantic unless he is captain. His salary is twice as much as Cunard captains', at £1,250 a year (that's 300 times as much as *Titanic*'s stewardesses are paid). It will be Smith's last voyage, as he is retiring.

## Members of the crew

**CAPTAIN SMITH.** He is in charge of 892 crew members, divided into three departments. The deck department is made up of 73 officers and seamen. The engine department has 325 crew and the stewards' department has 494.

*Captain*

**OFFICERS.** The officers are paid between £9 and £25 per month depending on length of service and experience.

*Officer*

**SEAMEN.** The able seamen are paid about £5 per month, depending on their duties. The deck crew works shifts of four hours on and eight hours off.

*Seaman*

12

If only we could get to New York in time to make the morning papers!

We don't want to force the engines when we are breaking them in, Mr Ismay.

**Handy hint** (for crew only)

Sluurrp

Be very nice to the passengers – tips can really boost your pay.

# The power of steam

**TRIPLE-SCREW STEAMER.** *Titanic* is a triple-screw (three-propeller) steamer with five engines. Steam is produced in the six boiler rooms and piped to the engine rooms. Once the steam has passed through the engines, it is piped to the condensers where it is cooled back into water and reused.

**STEWARDS AND STEWARDESSES.** Their duties and pay depend on which part of the ship they work in. Some wait on tables, others attend to cabins. One stewardess's monthly pay is about £3 and 15 shillings for working 17 hours a day.

*Stewardess and steward*

**CHEFS.** There are two onboard chefs who supervise the two kitchens and a total of 35 cooks.

**STOREKEEPERS.** There are two storekeepers with two assistants on board.

*Chef*

*Storekeeper*

# All aboard

*Manservant*  *Lady's maid*  *Nanny*

ow the crew can welcome passengers on board. There are three categories of passengers: First Class, Second Class and Steerage (Third Class). You will travel in First Class, naturally.

•R.M.S. TITANIC•
FIRST CLASS PASSAGE
TO NEW YORK
2 ADULTS
1 CHILD
3 SERVANTS
£151.16.0d

•R.M.S. TITANIC•
SECOND CLASS PASSAGE
TO NEW YORK
2 ADULTS
1 CHILD
£29.0.0d

First Class passengers travel in the most comfortable areas of the ship – the luxurious accommodation will attract the wealthy. Steerage passengers stay in the lower, less desirable parts of the ship. Many of these poorer passengers are emigrating to North America, looking for a new life.

STEERAGE. The accommodation in the Steerage section of the ship is basic compared to other sections of the liner. Single men and women in Steerage are separated by the entire length of the ship – men in the bow, women at the stern. Families are housed together in cabins.

• R.M.S. TITANIC •
THIRD CLASS PASSAGE
TO NEW YORK
2 ADULTS
2 CHILDREN
£24.17.0d

## Handy hint

(for millionaires only)

Try to reserve a stateroom with a 15-m-long private promenade deck. Book early to avoid disappointment – there are only two and they cost £880 each.

## Other travellers

There will be plenty of dogs on *Titanic*, so an informal dog show is being planned for Monday 15 April.

15

# Stocking the ship
## What you will need for a transatlantic crossing:

*Titanic's* food stores and equipment include 4,990 kg fresh fish, 1,800 kg dried fish, 3,402 kg bacon and ham, 11,340 kg poultry and game, 1,134 kg sausages, 6,820 litres of fresh milk, 44,000 pieces of cutlery, 29,000 items of glassware, 34,020 kg fresh meat, 40,000 fresh eggs, 40 tonnes of potatoes, 800 bundles of asparagus, 1,000 bottles of wine, 15,000 bottles of ale and stout, 12,000 dinner plates, 1,000 oyster forks, 15,000 champagne glasses, 40,000 towels, 45,000 table napkins, 5 grand pianos, 14 wooden lifeboats, 2 wooden cutters, 4 Englehardt collapsible boats, total lifeboat capacity 1,178 (Hold on, there are 2,206 passengers and crew! Never mind, the ship is 'unsinkable' after all...), 3,560 life-jackets, 49 life buoys.

Cargo list: Wakem & McLaughlin – 1 case wine, 25 case biscuits, 42 case wines. Spaulding & Brothers – 34 case athletic goods. Park & Tilford –1 case toothpaste, 5 case drug sundries, 1 case brushware. Maltus & Ware – 8 case orchids. Spencerian Pen Co. – 4 case pens. Sherman Sons & Co. – 7 case cotton. Claflin, H. B. & Co. – 12 case cotton lace. Muser Brothers – 3 case tissues. Isler & Guve – 4 bales straw. Rydeman & Lassner – 1 case Tulle (veil and scarf netting). Petry, P. H. & Co. – 1 case Tulle. Metzger, A. S. – 2 case Tulle. Mills & Gibb – 20 case cottons, 1 case gloves. Field, Marshall & Co. – 1 case gloves. NY Motion Pic. Co. – 1 case film. Thorburn, J. M. & Co. – 3 case bulbs. Rawstick Trading Co. – 28 bags sticks. Dujardin & Ladnick – 10 box melons. Tiffany & Co. – 1 cask china. Lustig Bros. – 4 case straw hats. Kuyper, P. C. & Co. – 1 case elastic cords, 1 case leather. Cohen, M. Bros. – 5 package skins. Gross, Engle Co. – 61 case Tulle. Gallia Textile Co. – 1 case lace goods. Calhoun, Robbins & Co. – 1 case cotton laces, ½ case brushware. Victor & Achiles – 1 case brushware. Baumgarten, Wm & Co. – 3 case furniture. Spielman Co. – 3 case silk crepe. Nottingham Lace Works – 2 case cotton. Naday & Fleisher – 1 case laces. Rosenthal, Leo J. & Co. – 4 case cotton. Leeming, T. & Co. – 7 case biscuits. Crown Perfume Co. – 3 case soap perfume. Meadows, T. & Co. – 5 case books, 3 box samples, 1 case parchment. Thomas & Pierson – 2 case hardware, 2 case books, 2 case furniture. American Express Co. – 1 case elastics, 1 case Edison gramophones, 4 case hosiery...

The ship's full name is RMS *Titanic* – the RMS stands for Royal Mail Ship, as she will be used for shipping mail between Britain and the United States. There is a rumour that gold bars are also on board – but gold is transported and recorded as 'mail' to keep it secret. *Titanic*'s huge hold is filled with all sorts of things, from walnuts to ostrich feathers. Some of the wealthy passengers are even taking cars with them.

Handy hint

Make sure all your items are insured. The total worth of the cargo on board *Titanic* in 1912 is £85,000.

BRYAN

# Watch out! Leaving Southampton
## Rich and famous on board

*John Jacob Astor IV*

*Benjamin Guggenheim*

*Mr & Mrs Isidor Straus*

*Colonel Archibald Gracie*

At 12.00 noon on 10 April 1912, *Titanic* sets off from Southampton. Swift action by Captain Smith avoids a collision with another ship docked there, the *New York*. *Titanic* reaches Cherbourg, France, at dusk, where the wealthiest of the passengers embark. On 11 April, *Titanic* arrives in Queenstown, Ireland, before setting off across the Atlantic.

MONEY, MONEY, MONEY. Among the First Class passengers is John Jacob Astor IV, the richest man on board. Benjamin Guggenheim's family made a fortune from mining, and Isidor Straus is the founder of Macy's department store in New York. Colonel Gracie's account of *Titanic's* maiden voyage will make him famous one day.

## Route to New York

Southampton

Queenstown

Cherbourg

Disaster strikes!

Planned route to New York

18

## Handy hint

Ignore the 1898 book *Futility*. It tells the tale of a ship sinking on its maiden voyage with many lives lost due to too few lifeboats.

The wash from *Titanic's* huge propellers causes the *New York* to break her moorings and pulls her straight into the path of the *Titanic* (below).

Oooh!

AAaargh!

# A tour of the ship

FIRST CLASS STATEROOMS. Working fireplaces are just one of the features in these lavishly decorated rooms. The rooms can accommodate one, two or three people.

Some of these First Class cabins have to share a bathroom!

Your designers and shipbuilders have done a wonderful job, especially with the First Class sections. The dining rooms are elegant and spacious and there are luxurious staterooms, cafés and libraries. The main forward staircase is one of the ship's most dramatic features, lit from above by natural

## First Class

Drone, drone, drone...

STEERAGE. Third Class passengers stay in four-berth cabins. These are rather comfortable and would be used in Second Class on other ships.

There are only two baths for the 710 passengers in Third Class!

light through a huge domed skylight. *Titanic* has three elevators in the First Class section and is the first ship to have one for Second Class passengers. She is also the first ocean liner to have a swimming pool and a gym. Although Second Class cabins are bigger and more luxurious than those in Steerage, they look small and bare compared to the sumptuous rooms on the higher decks.

Try out the exercise machines in the gymnasium in First Class. Passengers travelling in Second Class are allowed to look around First Class before the ship sets sail.

## Second Class

## Steerage (Third Class)

# Icebergs ahead...

*...the engines have never run so fast...*

Captain Smith is a guest of Mr and Mrs Widener at dinner in the restaurant on B deck.

*Another warning, Captain.*

He receives another message about icebergs – the sixth warning today.

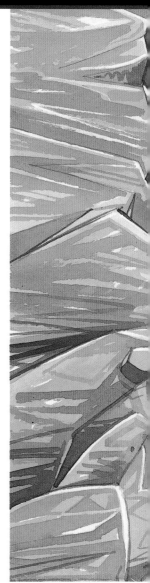

The ship is now steaming toward New York at speeds of more than 22.5 knots (42 kph) – so fast that she will arrive a day early. Ice warnings are coming in from other ships in this area of the North Atlantic. The lookout crew in the crow's-nest have been warned to watch out for icebergs – but their binoculars were left behind in Southampton! At 11.40 p.m., you are awoken by strange scraping noises. Putting a coat on over your pyjamas, you head for the ship's bridge. Captain Smith tells you the ship has struck ice and is seriously damaged, but you don't believe him.

*It's very cold, Officer Lightoller.*

*One degree above freezing, Sir.*

It is a moonless evening, and the sea is calm. Captain Smith leaves the bridge to go to bed at 9.20 p.m.

When the watch changes at 10.00 p.m., Officer Murdoch takes charge of the wheel on the bridge.

11.40 p.m. Lookouts spot an iceberg. The ship's engines are put into reverse, but it is too late and *Titanic* scrapes along the side.

**Crrrunch!**

Handy hint

Send emergency messages by Morse code. Use the traditional distress signal, CQD, and try the new one, SOS, because it is quicker and easier to send.

DAMAGE TO THE SHIP. Hitting the iceberg made the hull plates buckle. The water pressure on the weakened joints makes the rivets pop out and the plates are pushed apart.

We've struck an iceberg, sir!

11.50 p.m. Captain Smith returns to the bridge and orders the watertight doors to be closed. This will make the ship unsinkable.

Midnight You both inspect the ship. Water is gushing into the hull, flowing above the bulkheads and pulling the ship down.

Captain Smith faces the grim reality that his ship is sinking. The telegraph operator begins sending emergency messages.

23

# Wake up! Life-jackets on!

## What do you do?

PANIC?!

Stay calm...

...or stay in bed?!

Soon after midnight, Captain Smith orders the lifeboats to be prepared, and adds that women and children should evacuate *Titanic* before the men. The first lifeboat, number 7, splashes into the water at 12.25 a.m., 45 minutes after the collision. It contains 28 passengers, but has space for 65. By 1.20 a.m., six lifeboats have left the ship. Deep in the boiler and engine rooms, engineers and crew risk their own safety to keep the lights burning and the pumps working. You help people into the lifeboats, then quietly slip yourself into collapsible boat C.

COME BACK! Using a megaphone, Captain Smith orders several of the half-empty lifeboats to return to the ship to pick up more passengers. None respond because they are afraid of becoming overloaded.

SINKING? I DON'T BELIEVE IT. Few passengers believe that the ship is really sinking. The thought of descending into the darkness of the icy Atlantic makes many people stay on deck in the hope of being rescued. A lot of the female passengers refuse to be separated from their husbands.

# Sinking fast

## How *Titanic* sinks

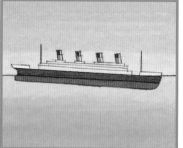

**BULKHEADS.** Six compartments are split open, and even the watertight doors cannot save the ship.

**FRONT FIRST.** The weight of the water in the front compartments pulls the bow of the ship downwards.

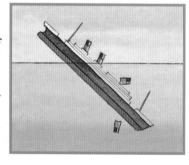

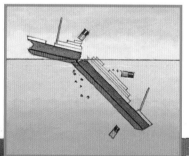

**BOW SUBMERGED.** The ship tears apart and the bow heads for the ocean floor.

**FINAL MINUTES.** The stern bobs upright for five minutes before filling with water and sinking.

By 2.15 a.m. on 15 April, fourteen lifeboats, two emergency boats and four collapsibles have left the ship. Over 1,500 people remain on board. *Titanic*'s stern begins to rise up out of the ocean. Water is pouring in through the open portholes. The ship's lights are still on and the band bravely continues to play on deck. At 2.18 a.m., the lights start to flicker off and on. Rivets begin to pop and deck planks snap as the ship begins to break in two. The noise is deafening. Once the bow is totally submerged it finally rips apart from the rest of the ship and plunges to the ocean floor. Just a few minutes later you turn your back as *Titanic*'s stern slides under the water. Captain Smith is last seen on the bridge, having given final orders to abandon ship.

TITANIC

## Handy hint

Help the crew of your lifeboat row away from the ship so you aren't sucked down with her when she sinks.

## Molly Brown

Mrs Margaret Brown becomes known as the 'Unsinkable Molly Brown' for taking command of lifeboat number 6 and demanding that women should be allowed to row as well as men.

# The aftermath

Only one person is rescued alive from the freezing sea. Over 1,500 lives are lost, but only 306 of those bodies are picked up. The dead from First Class are embalmed and taken home for burial, but those from Third Class and crew members are sewn up in heavy linen and buried at sea. The wages of the 214 surviving crew are calculated and paid up to the moment the ship sank.

At the official inquiries that follow, many questions are asked: should *Titanic* have been sailing more slowly? Should she have carried more lifeboats? After the disaster, a change in the law ensures that all passenger ships carry enough lifeboats for everyone on board and that regular lifeboat drills are held. All ships also have to have 24-hour radio watch.

They are frozen to death, not drowned.

There's someone alive!

# SS Carpathia to the rescue

## What happens to you?

J. BRUCE ISMAY. What has happened to J. Bruce Ismay, the man who dreamed of building the greatest liners in the world? You have survived the disaster, but your reputation is ruined. Within a year you resign from the White Star Line and donate a large sum of money to the pensions fund for widows of *Titanic* crew. You die in 1937 at the age of 74, having never made any further public statement about *Titanic* since the inquiries into the disaster.

SS CARPATHIA. This Cunard ship is 93 km away from *Titanic* when she receives the SOS signal. She steams to the scene of the disaster and arrives at 4.10 a.m.

SURVIVORS TAKEN TO NEW YORK. *Carpathia* cruises the area looking for any last survivors before setting sail for New York with 705 of *Titanic*'s stunned passengers on board.

# Glossary

**Berth**  A fixed bunk on a ship for sleeping in, or a ship's place in dock.

**Bow**  The front end of a boat or ship.

**Bridge**  The place on a ship where the captain and officers control every other part of the ship.

**Bulkhead**  An upright partition separating the compartments of a ship.

**Collapsible boat**  A type of lifeboat that is folded up and stored until needed.

**Commodore**  The senior captain of a shipping line.

**CQD**  The standard ship distress call, first used in 1903. 'CQ' was the signal for listening radio operators to stop and pay attention; adding the 'D' meant distress.

**Crow's-nest**  A shelter or platform high up the mast of a ship for a lookout person.

**Dry dock**  An area for building or repairing ships, from which water can be pumped out.

**Emigrant**  A person who leaves his or her own country to go and live in another.

**Hull**  The body or frame of a ship.

**Keel**  The 'backbone' of a ship along which the rest of the hull is built up.

**Mooring**  A fixed object that a ship can be tied to.

**Morse code**  A set of dots, dashes and spaces used to send messages via radio to other ships or to land.

**Porthole**  A window in the side of a ship.

**Rivet**  A metal device for holding sheets of metal together.

**SOS**  The Morse code distress signal that came into official use in 1908. The three dots, three dashes and three dots are quick and easy to recognise and send.

**Steerage**  The part of a ship with accommodation for passengers with the cheapest tickets, or Third Class.

**Stern**  The back end of a boat or ship.

**Transatlantic**  Spanning across the Atlantic Ocean.

**Ventilation**  The forced movement of air around a room or rooms.

**Waterline**  The line along which the surface of water touches the side of a ship.

# Index

## A
anchors 7, 8, 11
Astor, John Jacob IV 18

## B
boilers 7, 10–11, 13, 24
bow 15, 26, 30
*Britannic* 6
Brown, Margaret 'Molly' 27
bulkheads 8, 23, 26, 30

## C
cabins 13, 15, 20
cargo 16–17
*Carpathia* 29
chefs 13
Cherbourg, France 18
collapsible boats 7, 16, 24, 26, 30
condensers 13
CQD 23, 30
crew 10, 11, 12–13, 14, 22, 24, 27, 28, 29
crow's-nest 22, 30
Cunard 5, 12, 29

## D
decks 8, 12, 15, 21, 22, 24, 26
dining rooms 20
dogs 15
dry docks 6, 8, 30

## E
electricians 10
elevators 21
emigrants 5, 30
engineers 10, 24
engines 11, 12, 13, 22, 24

## F
firemen 10
First Class 14, 18, 20, 21, 28
food 16
funnels 7, 11

## G
Gracie, Colonel Archibald 18
greaser 10
Guggenheim, Benjamin 18
gym 21

## H
Harland and Wolff 5, 6, 8
hull 7, 8, 10, 23, 30

## I
ice warnings 22
icebergs 22–23
Ismay, J. Bruce 5, 6, 13, 29

## K
keel 6, 8, 31
kitchens 13

## L
libraries 20
lifeboats 7, 16, 19, 24–25, 26–27, 28
life-jackets 16, 24
*Lusitania* 5

## M
Morse code 23, 31

## N
New York 18, 22, 29
*New York* (ship) 18–19

## O
officers 12, 22
*Olympic* 6

## P
portholes 26, 31
propellers 7, 9, 13, 19

## Q
Queenstown, Ireland 18

## R
riveters 8–9
rivets 8–9, 23, 26, 31
rudder 7

## S
seamen 12
Second Class 14, 20, 21
ship's bridge 22, 23, 26, 30
ship's hold 16
shipyard 8–9, 10
Smith, Captain E. J. 12, 18, 22–23, 24, 26
SOS 23, 29, 31
Southampton, England 18, 22
Steerage 14–15, 20, 21, 28, 31
stern 15, 26, 31
stewards/stewardesses 12, 13
stoker 10, 11
storekeepers 13
Straus, Isidor 18
swimming pool 21

## T
Third Class (*see* Steerage)
trimmers 10

## W
waterline 8, 31
White Star Line 5, 6, 10, 29

# Top Titanic tourist sites

**Halifax, Nova Scotia, Canada**  One hundred and fifty *Titanic* victims were buried in Halifax, and visitors can explore the Mount Olivet and Fairlawn Cemeteries where the *Titanic* graves are marked by a display. There is also an exhibition on the *Titanic* in Halifax's Maritime Museum of the Atlantic. It includes artefacts such as a deck chair pulled from the water in the weeks after the sinking.

**Denver, Colorado, USA**  Here you can visit the home of famous *Titanic* survivor Molly Brown.

**New York, New York, USA**  Outside the South Street Seaport Museum you can see the *Titanic* Memorial, an 18 m (59 foot) lighthouse built in 1913. It was funded by donations raised through a campaign supported by survivor Molly Brown. There is also a memorial statue to victims Isidor and Ida Straus at 106th Street and Broadway.

**Liverpool, England**  There is a gallery dedicated to the *Titanic* disaster at the Merseyside Maritime Museum.

**London, England**  The White Star Line's London offices, named Oceanic House, still exist today, on Cockspur Street, just a short walk from Trafalgar Square.

**Belfast, Northern Ireland**  The spectacular *Titanic* Belfast museum opened in 2012, in Belfast's 'Titanic Quarter'. Guided boat tours take in the Harland and Wolff shipyards, including the famous Thompson Dock where the *Titanic* was built, and the *Titanic* Drawing Rooms where the designs were drawn up. At the Hamilton Graving Dock you can visit SS *Nomadic*, which ferried passengers to the *Titanic* at Cherbourg. It is the only surviving White Star Line ship.

# Did you know?

In Belfast you can buy a T-shirt giving the city's take on the disaster: 'She was alright when she left here!'

# Trouble at sea

**Shortcut** Bound for Jakarta in Indonesia, the *Tek Sing* left the port of Amoy (now Xiamen in Fujian, China) packed with porcelain and Chinese emigrants. A month into the voyage, the captain, Io Tauko, decided to chance a shortcut through the Gaspar Strait. On 6 February 1822, the *Tek Sing* struck a reef and sank within the hour, in about 30 m (98 feet) of water. Around 1,600 people went down with the ship.

**Fire** On 15 June 1904, the paddle steamer *General Slocum* caught fire in New York's East River. All told, more than 1,000 people died – mostly women and children on their way to a picnic – making it New York's worst disaster until the 9/11 attacks in 2001. It was later found that the firm that made the life jackets had filled them with cheap, useless material instead of cork, then added iron bars to make them the correct weight! Anyone who strapped on one of these jackets and jumped into the water quickly sank to the bottom.

**Typhoon** The Japanese steamship SS *Kiche Maru* sank during a typhoon in the Pacific Ocean on 22 September 1912. More than 1,000 people lost their lives. Since there were no survivors, very little is known about what actually happened. The storm sank hundreds of vessels and devastated the ports of Osaka and Nagoya.

**Torpedoed** The liner RMS *Lusitania* was torpedoed without warning by a German U-boat (submarine) on 7 May 1915, and sank in 18 minutes off the southwest coast of Ireland. Two explosions rocked the ship. The first was caused by the torpedo, but a second, much larger explosion has never been fully explained – was the *Lusitania* secretly carrying armaments? An estimated 1,198 people died, including 139 US citizens. The attack eventually led to the United States declaring war on Germany.

**Fog**  The French steamer *La Bourgogne* sank on 4 July 1898, after the British sailing ship *Cromartyshire* accidentally rammed her in dense fog off Cape Sable, Nova Scotia. Five hundred and sixty-five lives were lost. Survivors described brutal scenes as the crew of the French ship grabbed all available lifeboats and rafts. Panic broke out, with passengers using knives and revolvers in a mad rush to recapture the lifeboats.

**Bad navigation**  On the night of 22 October 1707, a Royal Navy fleet returning from Gibraltar to Portsmouth, England, sailed through dangerous reefs off the Isles of Scilly. Four ships – HMS *Association, Eagle, Romney* and *Firebrand* – sank and more than 1,500 sailors died. Their bodies washed up on shore for days afterward.

**Snow**  On 24 March 1878, the training vessel HMS *Eurydice* was caught in a heavy snowstorm off the Isle of Wight, near the south coast of England. The sailing ship capsized and sank, and those who survived the sinking soon froze to death in the icy waters. Just two of the ship's 366 crew and trainees survived.

**Sharks, salt and thirst**  On 30 July 1945, the USS *Indianapolis* was torpedoed by a Japanese submarine and sank in 12 minutes. Around 300 crew members went down with the ship. The remaining 880 floated in the water, waiting for help. But the US Navy did not know about the sinking for another four days. By then, hundreds more had died from cold, lack of food and water, salt poisoning and shark attacks. Only 317 of the 1,196 crew survived. This was the greatest single loss of life at sea in the history of the US Navy.